FILL IN THE BLANK FOR KIDS WORKBOOK

Grade 1 - 3 Edition

Speedy Publishing LLC
40 E. Main St. #1156
Newark, DE 19711
www.speedypublishing.com

Vocabulary Exercises

Cut and Paste

Name: ____________________ Score: ____________

Fill in the blanks with the correct letter. Cut and paste the images beside the words.

1. 

2. 

3. 

4. 

For Cutting Purposes Only

Name: ______________________________ Score: ______________

Fill in the blanks with the correct letter. Cut and paste the images beside the words.

For Cutting Purposes Only

Exercise No. 3

Name: ______________________________ Score: ____________________

Fill in the blanks with the correct letter. Cut and paste the images beside the words.

1. P_ncil

2. Rock_t

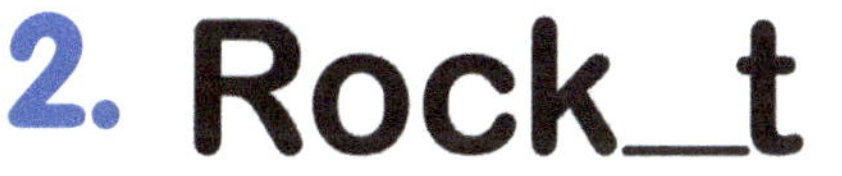

3. Not_

4. Or_ng_

For Cutting Purposes Only

Name: ____________________ Score: ____________

Fill in the blanks with the correct letter. Cut and paste the images beside the words.

1. Y_cht

2. L_mp

3. Xylophon_

4. Wh_l_

For Cutting Purposes Only

Name: ______________________ Score: ______________

Fill in the blanks with the correct letter. Cut and paste the images beside the words.

1. fi_h 

2. ba_ 

3. vas_ 

4. g_ft 

For Cutting Purposes Only

Exercise No. 6

Name: ______________________________ Score: ____________________

Fill in the blanks with the correct letter. Cut and paste the images beside the words.

1. dr _ m

2. r_bo_

3. que_ _

4. _oc_s

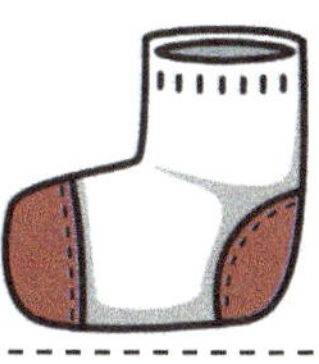

For Cutting Purposes Only

Exercise No. 7

Name: ______________________ Score: ______________

Fill in the blanks with the correct letter. Cut and paste the images beside the words.

1. lad_b_g

2. _ird

3. pe__ut

4. ro_k_t

For Cutting Purposes Only

Name: ______________________ Score: ______________

Fill in the blanks with the correct letter. Cut and paste the images beside the words.

1. hou_e

2. ju_c_

3. i_lo_

4. i_e cre__

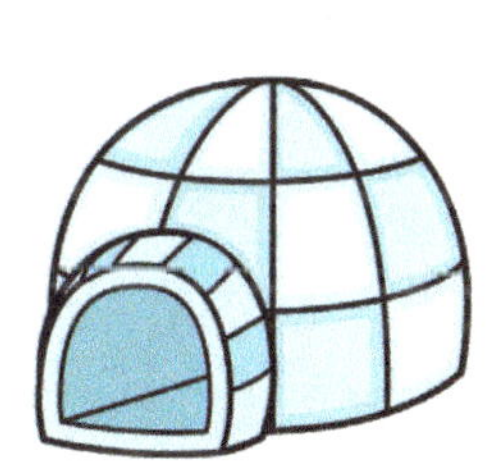

Name: ________________________________ Score: ______________

Fill in the blanks with the correct letter. Cut and paste the images beside the words.

1. mou_e

2. isla_d

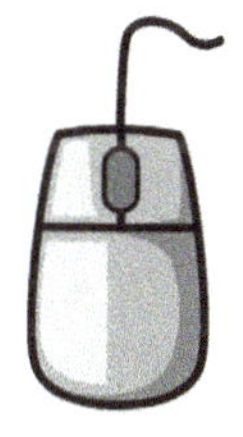

3. s_u_sh

4. to_ _to

For Cutting Purposes Only

Fill in the blanks

Exercise No. 1

Name: ______________________________ Score: ______________

Fill in the blanks with the correct letter.

1.  bro___

2. 

blo___

3.  cr___

4.  dr___

5.  tr___

6.  fr___

Exercise No. 2

Name: ______________________________ Score: ________________

Fill in the blanks with the correct letter.

1.  ch__se

4.  b__t

2.  cl__n

5.  back__e

3.  sc__ol

6. 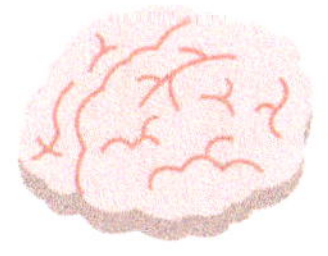 br_in

 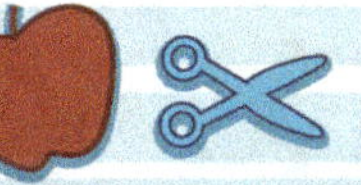     

Exercise No. 3

Name: ______________________ Score: ______________

Fill in the blanks with the correct letter.

1.  gra___

4.   sca___

2.  glo___

5.  ska___

3.  pret__l

6.  slipp___

Exercise No. 4

Name: ______________________________ Score: ______________

Fill in the blanks with the correct letter.

1.  pho___

4.  w__ch

2.  kni___

5.  ri___

3.  que___

6.  ___ll

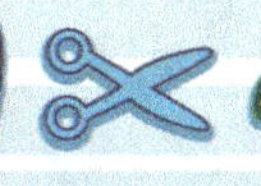

Exercise No. 5

Name: ______________________________ Score: ______________

Fill in the blanks with the correct letter.

1.  ___ug

2.  ___ench

3.  ___ck

4.  ___ock

5.  ___ugh

6.  ___uirrel

 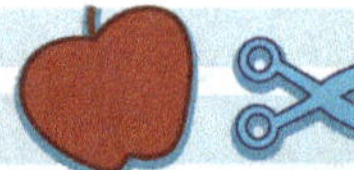      

Exercise No. 6

Name: ________________________________ Score: ________________

Fill in the blanks with the correct letter.

1.  ____ etzel

4.  ____ irt

2.  ____ ug

5. 

____ hool

3.   ____ ess

6.  ____ arf

Exercise No. 7

Name: ______________________ Score: ______________

Fill in the blanks with the correct letter.

1.  ____ ane

4. 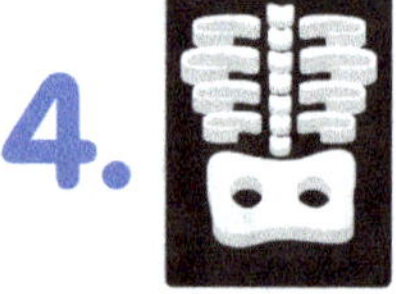 ____ eleton

2.  ____ ume

5.  ____ an

3.  ____ incess

6.  ____ ig

Exercise No. 8

Name: ______________________________ Score: ______________

Fill in the blanks with the correct letter.

1. 

____ ock

2. ____ ain

3. ____ own

4. 
____ ayon

5. 

____ ock

6. 
____ oud

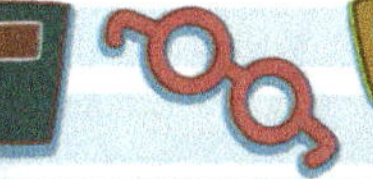

Exercise No. 9

Name: ____________________ Score: ____________

Fill in the blanks with the correct letter.

1.  ___ anket

2. ___ ue

3. ___ ush

4.  ___ ab

5.  ___ own

6.  ___ ean

Exercise No. 10

Name: ______________________________ Score: ________________

Fill in the blanks with the correct letter.

1. ____ozen

2. ____ag

3. ____uit

4. ____obe

5. ____ove

6. ____ape

Exercise No. 11

Name: ______________________ Score: ______________

Fill in the blanks with the correct letter.

1.  ____ og

2.  ____ ower

3.  ____ y

4.  ____ ocery

5.  ____ ass

6.  ____ ass

Fill in the blanks

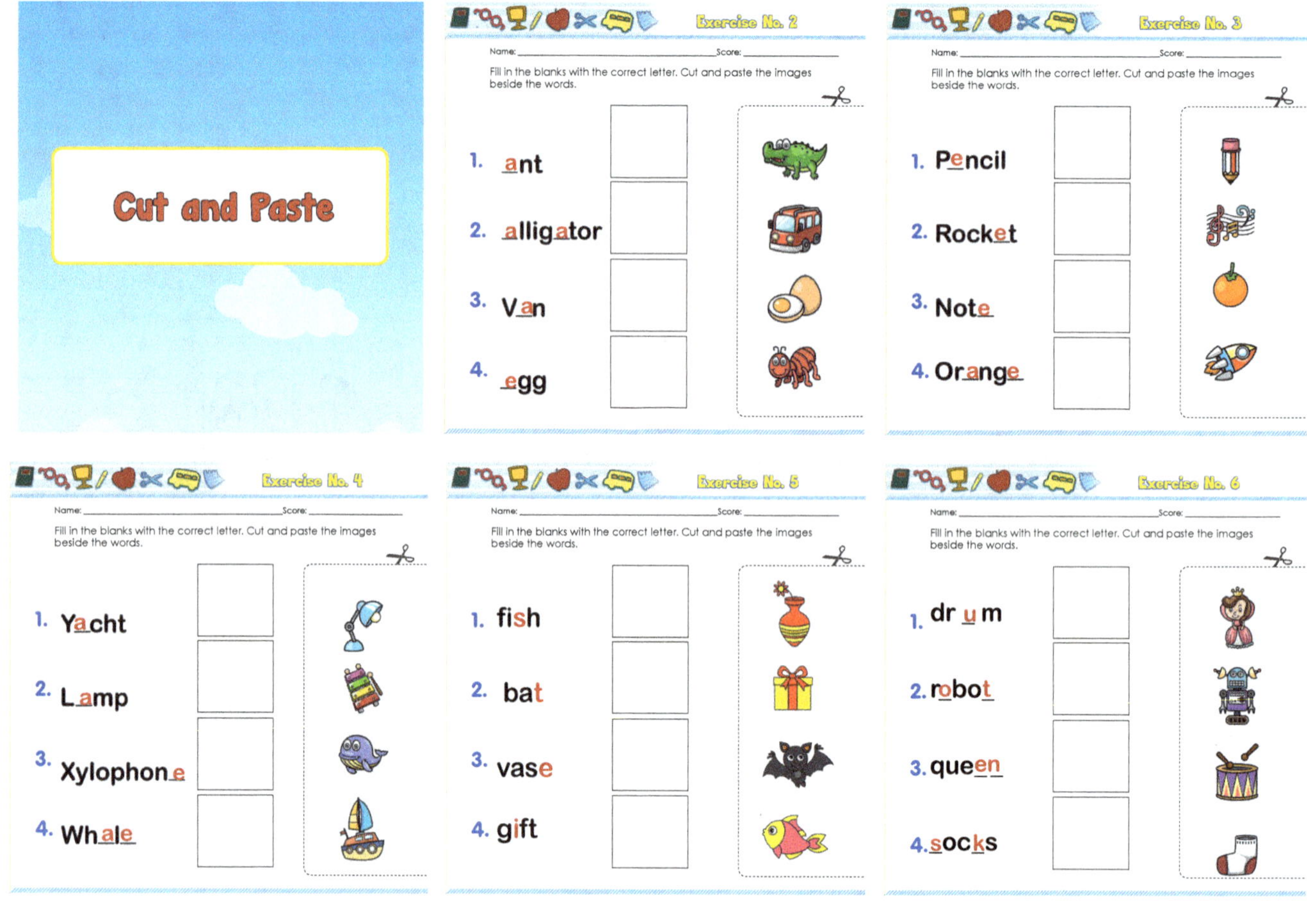

Cut and Paste

Exercise No. 2

Name: ______________________ Score: ____________

Fill in the blanks with the correct letter. Cut and paste the images beside the words.

1. ant
2. alligator
3. Van
4. egg

Exercise No. 3

Name: ______________________ Score: ____________

Fill in the blanks with the correct letter. Cut and paste the images beside the words.

1. Pencil
2. Rocket
3. Note
4. Orange

Exercise No. 4

Name: ______________________ Score: ____________

Fill in the blanks with the correct letter. Cut and paste the images beside the words.

1. Yacht
2. Lamp
3. Xylophone
4. Whale

Exercise No. 5

Name: ______________________ Score: ____________

Fill in the blanks with the correct letter. Cut and paste the images beside the words.

1. fish
2. bat
3. vase
4. gift

Exercise No. 6

Name: ______________________ Score: ____________

Fill in the blanks with the correct letter. Cut and paste the images beside the words.

1. dr u m
2. robot
3. queen
4. socks

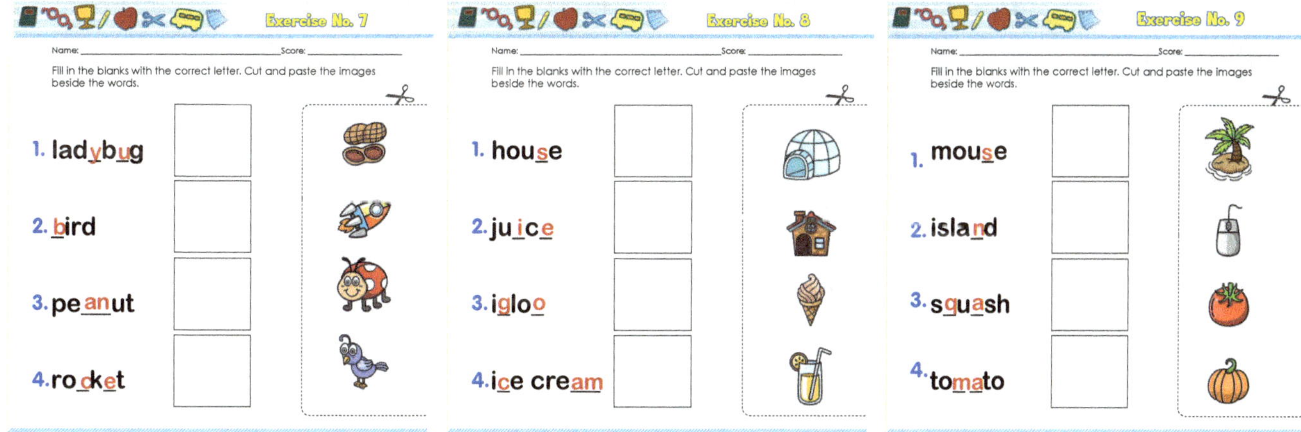

Exercise No. 7

Name: ____________________ Score: __________

Fill in the blanks with the correct letter. Cut and paste the images beside the words.

1. ladybug
2. bird
3. peanut
4. rocket

Exercise No. 8

Name: ____________________ Score: __________

Fill in the blanks with the correct letter. Cut and paste the images beside the words.

1. house
2. juice
3. igloo
4. ice cream

Exercise No. 9

Name: ____________________ Score: __________

Fill in the blanks with the correct letter. Cut and paste the images beside the words.

1. mouse
2. island
3. squash
4. tomato

Exercise No. 1

Name: ____________________ Score: __________

Fill in the blanks with the correct letter.

1. brown
2. blocks
3. cr ab
4. drum
5. tr uck
6. fr uit

Exercise No. 2

Name: ____________________ Score: __________

Fill in the blanks with the correct letter.

1. chee se
2. cl ean
3. school
4. boa t
5. backhoe
6. brain

Exercise No. 3

Name: ____________________ Score: __________

Fill in the blanks with the correct letter.

1. grass
2. gloves
3. pretze l
4. scam
5. skate
6. slipper

Exercise No. 4

Name: ____________________ Score: __________

Fill in the blanks with the correct letter.

1. photo
2. kni fe
3. queen
4. wat ch
5. ring
6. ball

Exercise No. 5

Name: ____________________ Score: __________

Fill in the blanks with the correct letter.

1. pl ug
2. wr ench
3. du ck
4. sm ock
5. la ugh
6. sq uirrel

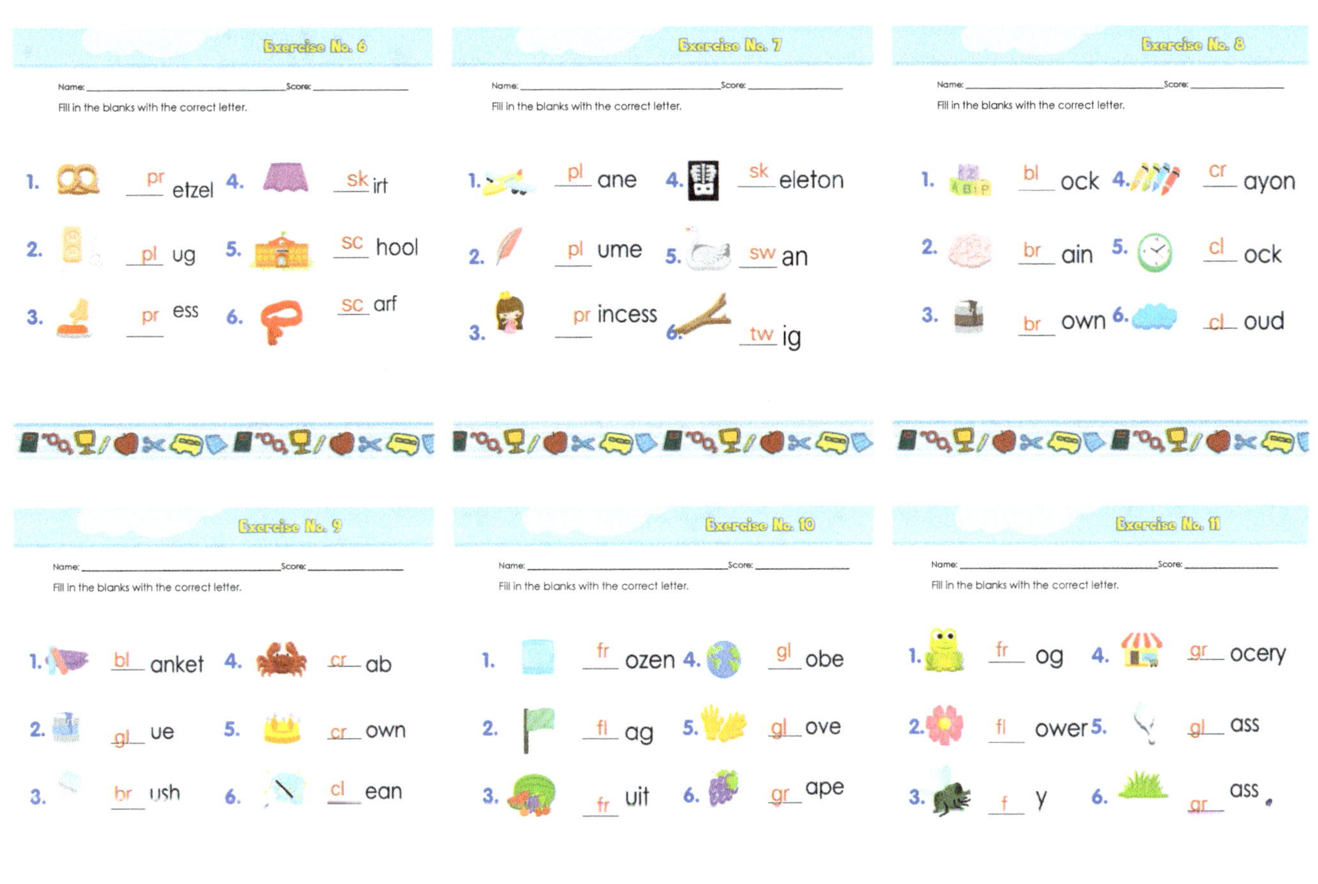

Exercise No. 6

Name: ______________________ Score: __________

Fill in the blanks with the correct letter.

1. pr etzel
2. pl ug
3. pr ess
4. sk irt
5. sc hool
6. sc arf

Exercise No. 7

Name: ______________________ Score: __________

Fill in the blanks with the correct letter.

1. pl ane
2. pl ume
3. pr incess
4. sk eleton
5. sw an
6. tw ig

Exercise No. 8

Name: ______________________ Score: __________

Fill in the blanks with the correct letter.

1. bl ock
2. br ain
3. br own
4. cr ayon
5. cl ock
6. cl oud

Exercise No. 9

Name: ______________________ Score: __________

Fill in the blanks with the correct letter.

1. bl anket
2. gl ue
3. br ush
4. cr ab
5. cr own
6. cl ean

Exercise No. 10

Name: ______________________ Score: __________

Fill in the blanks with the correct letter.

1. fr ozen
2. fl ag
3. fr uit
4. gl obe
5. gl ove
6. gr ape

Exercise No. 11

Name: ______________________ Score: __________

Fill in the blanks with the correct letter.

1. fr og
2. fl ower
3. f y
4. gr ocery
5. gl ass
6. gr ass

www.ingramcontent.com/pod-product-compliance
Lightning Source LLC
LaVergne TN
LVHW082307150826
845677LV00009B/1737
9798869442215